BOXER'S SHORTS

More than just a Brief attempt at Humor

3

THE MEDICAL VERSION

For Everyone in the Healing Arts and Sciences,
and their Patients and Clients,— i.e. For Anyone
Looking for a Healthy Laugh or Chuckle

Boxer's Shorts 3

THE MEDICAL VERSION

(More Than Just A Brief) Attempt At Humor

Punchline Press
Wilmette, Illinois

CREATED BY ROBERT BOXER M.D.
ILLUSTRATED BY DARNELL TOWNS

Book and Cover Design
Darnell Towns/Robert Boxer

Typesetting and Production Services
Sans Serif, Inc.

Cover Illustration
Darnell Towns

Back Cover Photograph
Arkady Rapoport, (an Innocent Bystander)

Back Cover Photograph Computer Manipulation
Michael Shaneyfelt

Published by Punchline Press
P.O. Box 6058, Wilmette, Illinois 60091

Printed in the United States of America

First Edition, April, 2001

Library of Congress Catalog Number 00-091733
ISBN: 0-9620687-2-1

Contents

DARNELL TOWNS 2000

Dedication

To physicians, fellows in training, residents, interns, medical students, physicians' assitants, nurses, student nurses, nurse's aides, medical technologists, office and hospital staffs and volunteers, hospital administrators, dentists, dental assistants and hygienists, veterinarians, podiatrists, optometrists, nutritionists, paramedics, E.M.T. technicians, pharmacists and pharmaceutical company representatives, and all others in the healing arts and sciences, and their patients, past, present, and future. This book is also dedicated to the many benefactors who have made contributions, both small and large, to hospitals, medical schools, and research institutions, as well as to all the researchers in the healing sciences whose efforts have helped to make remarkable progress.

Illustrator's Dedication

First of all, I would like to give God the glory and praise for blessing me with such a special gift. To all of my family whom have given me all of the love and support I could ever need.

Foreword

For over 25 years, the Boxer family has been an integral part of our family. During that time, Bob has been a trusted friend, has been our physician, and has enriched our lives with his characteristic kindness and good humor. Through Bob, we have come to know Darnell Towns, a very talented illustrator and a genuinely funny guy. Together, Bob and Darnell have created hundreds of word/picture puns that delight the mind and rattle the belly. Here now, is the third book resulting from this fun-loving collaboration.

Long before alternative medicine became the rage, Bob realized the therapeutic value that humor plays in medicine—indeed, that laughter truly is the best medicine! It therefore comes as no surprise that Bob's friends and patients have delighted in reading *Boxer Shorts* and *Boxer Shorts Round 2* in their homes and while sitting in Bob's waiting room. Now Bob is letting his colleagues in the medical profession in on the fun by publishing this collection of predominantly medical-related puns. Not being fully conversant in the medical arts, I had to ask Bob to explain to me a few of the puns in this book. This was all the more enjoyable because I was able to savor the illustrations, and then smile again as Bob explained the verbal puns to me. Notwithstanding the medical bent of this book, there is something here for everyone. Thankfully, Bob and Darnell have done it again.

William H. Frankel
Chicago, Illinois
June 2000

Preface

This third book of pun cartoons, conceived by myself and illustrated again by Darnell Towns, is devoted to pun cartoons that have to do with the healing arts, including humor regarding physicians, their patients, nurses and technicians, hospital staff, nutritionists, dentists, podiatrists, veterinarians, paramedics, and all of the other fine people involved in the various aspects of the healing arts. The humor should appeal to everyone, which means not only the professionals but also their patients or clients. Although veterinarians are importantly included in the healing arts, I have yet to find a pet, as lovable and intelligent as some are, who has been able to actually read and appreciate my humor.

Those who have read our earlier two books are aware that my penchant is visualization of situations lending themselves to illustration as pun cartoons, and Darnell has the unique ability to translate this humor in an artful form.

All of the work created in this book, as in the other books, is original in the sense that I have not heard nor seen the humor previously spoken nor drawn in a similar context. I suspect no one can be aware of all that has preceded, and surely similar ideas must arise simultaneously. Therefore, original in this sense means not knowingly incited nor stimulated by the work or thoughts of others.

This book does incorporate several cartoons from the first two books in this series, and also incorporates some of the cartoons that had appeared

monthly in *THE MAIN EVENT, A MONTHLY SPORTS JOURNAL FOR PHYSICIANS.* The cartoons created for *THE MAIN EVENT* incorporated sports and medical themes.

As with our previous works, I hope that our readers enjoy the blending of original humor and art that we have put together in this collection.

"DON'T WORRY. I HAVE AN AUTO IMMUNE DISEASE."

1

"THIS IS NOT EXACTLY WHAT I HAD IN MIND WHEN I ASKED ABOUT A SHRINK WRAPPER."

2

"No Dear, I'm not on my mobile phone, but I am stuck in the middle of a bridge."

3

"No, those aren't the tablets I told you to take."

"Does that sign outside mean I can only get 35 tablets of Dextro-amphetamine at a time?

created by Robert Boxer M.D.   Illustrated by Darnell Towns

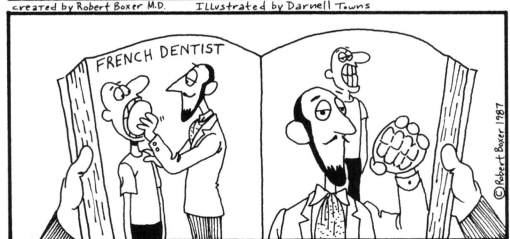

"I'm sorry. We can't today. We're really swamped".

"I'M JACK SHEEP. I'M HERE TO SEE DR. SMITH ABOUT A RE-FUR-RAL."

"Doctor Peters, can you see me today—
I seem to have lost my crown."

Created by Robert Boxer M.D.
Illustrated by Darnell Towns

9

"With your diplomatic immunity,
I'm surprised you caught it."

"THE HOSPITAL PATHOLOGISTS ARE SITTING IN THE FROZEN SECTION."

11

"THIS HOSPITAL IS NOTORIOUS FOR GHOST SURGERY."

"Yes, the official report is correct, it was no fluke".

14

"Well Doctor, you did ask me to design a low key office for you".

"Just watch him manipulate his way to the top."

"This will be a great GAG gift for our hospital party."

17

"Tell the doctor my infant son is having projectile vomiting."

"How long have you considered yourself a sex symbol?"

'Dr. Smith is just trying to put his patient on a mood elevator.'

20

"The Supervisor told me I'd
have to float this week".

"I suspect Dr. Jones will come up with his usual Wastebasket diagnosis".

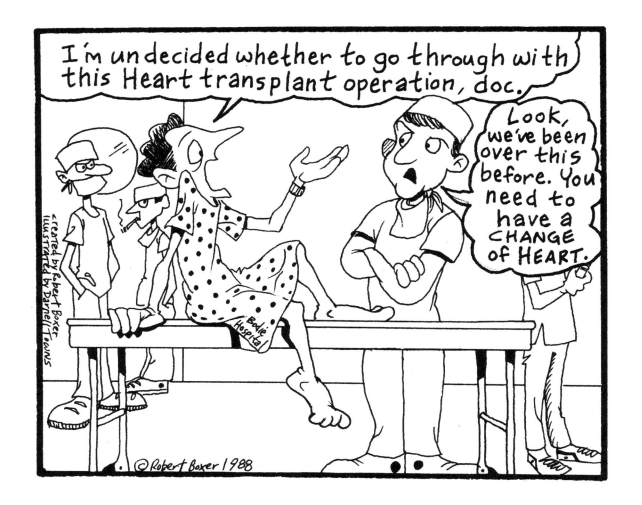

25

HARE ANALYSIS

"Doctor Thymus, Our Endocrinologist, always starts with T3 and T4"

"A Classic case of Mercury Poisoning".

"Wow! You must be an expert on **Unbundling**."

31

"My Son forgets to flush the Toliet, I heard Niacin will make you flush."

"I suppose you would all like to see Sample Rooms".

"Well, her concern was about getting lead from Cookware. Definitely not your Average Crock."

"Here comes Mr. Smith with
his Vitamin B complex".

"Honey, that's not what the
Insurance Company meant by a second
opinion."

"Doctor, I thought that when I signed your **Operative** release it said I might become **IMPORTANT**."

"Doctors excuse? No way; for me my doctor said that this would be a <u>Therapeutic Trial</u>."

"Man, do I have disc problems."

Nurse: "Doctor, are you able to reach the foreign body?"
Doctor: "No problem, it's a piece of cake."

"Nurse, You know what to do with this F.B.I. mole."

"For Sunday's Football game, I'm on call, so please get me two seats in the C-section".

"Let me show you my BUTTERFLY COLLECTION."

45

"He definitely is a socialite allergist,
he only treats 'status asthmaticus'."

"NOT YOUR USUAL HOSPITAL TURF BATTLE."

48

"Is this what the text book meant by 'Terminal Illness?'"

"During Hay Fever season, to go through two
boxes of tissue a day is nothing."

51

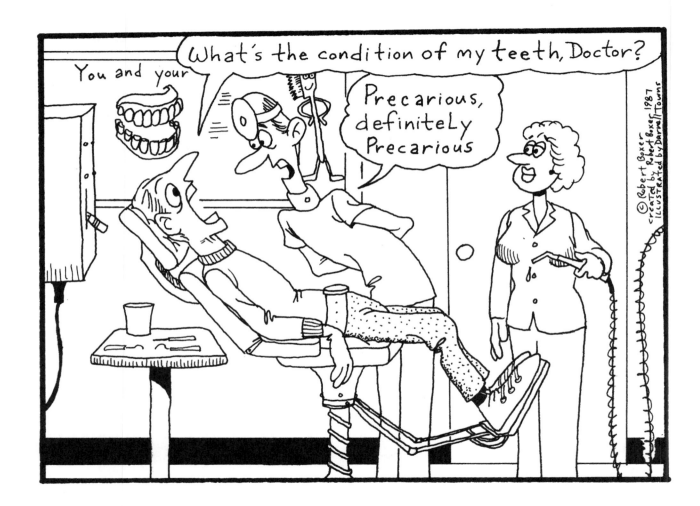

52

"I'M HERE BECAUSE YOU ARE A WORLD RENOWNED EXPERT IN LYME DISEASE."

"My friend said that I would be able to get rid of my hang-ups here".

"Do you have the new PET scanner that I've been reading about".

"The side effects of Antihistamines can be mind boggling".

59

"Maybe you're allergic to Cello mold".

A FREUDIAN SLIP

"HE REALLY HAD NO INTEREST IN POLITICS UNTIL HE WAS TOLD THAT HE WAS A CANDIDATE FOR ELECTIVE SURGERY."

"It looks like you've got a Nervous Tick."

"I hope you're not allergic, you just won the office kitty".

"These days in medicine, no matter what you pick, You'll still probably end up in a suit".

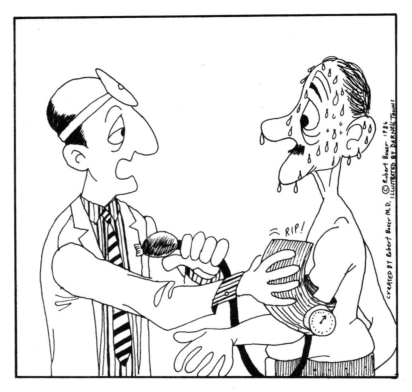

"I did'nt mean to worry you
about your blood pressure, it was
just an off the cuff remark".

"That's the twelfth time that guy rented Jaws II. He's an orthodontist, you know."

"Wow! This must be the famous Silicone Valley!"

A Low grade infection.

JUDGE: 'Aren't you the doctor who did open heart surgery on me several years ago?'

DOCTOR: 'No, your honor. I've never been in your chambers before.'

75

"Don't worry, Private, this discharge is not dishonorable."

"I SEE THE PROBLEM IS YOU'RE ALL WRAPPED UP IN YOURSELF."

"No, I'm afraid you have the wrong party. Perhaps you should call your doctor".

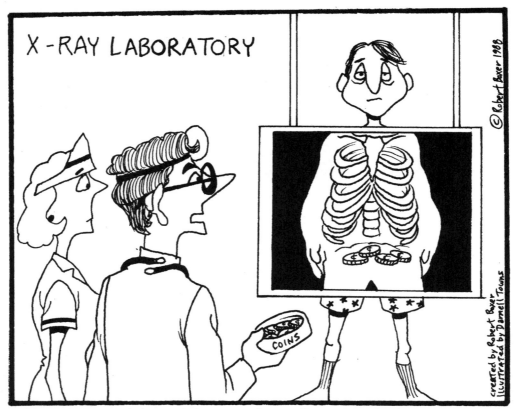

"For us, the policy of ordering X-rays on all coin swallowings makes a lot of cents."

"I guess you found out that Dr. Smith
is an expert on Contact Dermatitis".

"As the President of Puritan Oats,
I want you to know that this whole talk goes
against my grain."

"I warned you that if you kept giving the cold shoulder to everyone that you'd end up with it frozen."

"This Slide shows the response induced in these Animal Models".

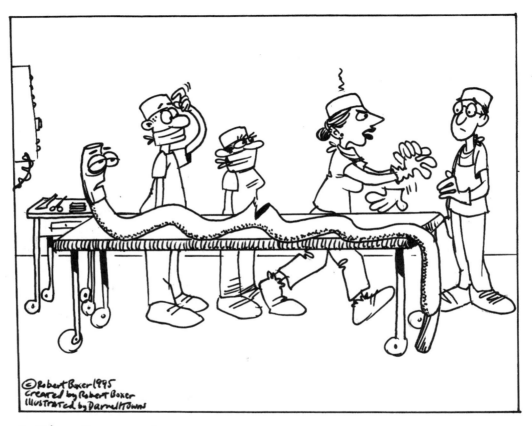

"I'VE TOLD THE HOSPITAL ADMINISTRATOR THAT WE CAN'T OPERATE ON A SHOESTRING."

"Here is one place where a positive attitude is not always a great thing."

"I WENT INTO PSYCHIATRY BECAUSE IN MEDICAL SCHOOL THEY SAID URI's WERE THE MOST COMMON ILLNESS. I THOUGHT THEY WERE REFERRING TO IDENTITY CRISES."

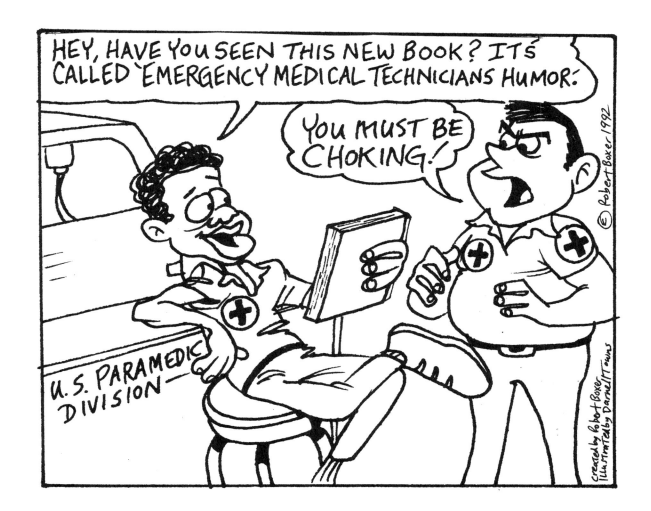

"Capitation, no way, I'm for **Decapitation**."

92

93

"We could hire you as a Medical Illustrator part time but if you're looking for a full-time position, maybe you could also draw blood."

"I think you're just suffering from
separation anxiety."

"HEY DOC, GOT ANYTHING TO STOP THIS ERUPTION?"

CREATED BY Robert Boxer M.D.
ILLUSTRATED BY DARNELL TOWNS

© Robert Boxer 1986

"No Dad, you don't have to go down to help treat anyone, P.A.T. means Point After Touchdown".

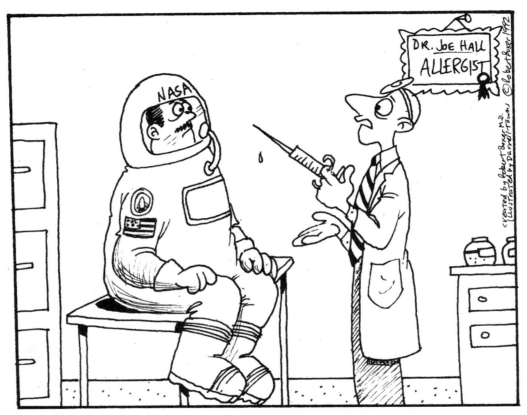

"COMMANDER, YOU'RE HAVING AN ALLERGIC REACTION. I'M GOING TO PUT YOU ON A CORTICOSTEROID COUNTDOWN."

"Yes Sheriff, I am considered an expert on the apprehension of criminals, but I can't help you capture escaped prisoners".

"This wasn't really what I had in mind when I signed up for a Rotating Internship."

"Ever since the cardiology conference he's been concerned about too many **plaques** on his **walls.**"

103

"You've got to learn to be less EXPLOSIVE!"

"Our next play is about the Reconstructionist Era after the Civil War. Is our plastic surgeon here tonight?"

"We're so impressed with how quickly you came up with the pun cartoon on the topic we suggested and how well he drew it that we were wondering if there were plants in the audience."

"OUR SPEAKER, DR. CATHETER WILL DISCUSS 'HOW TO DEVELOP A SOUND PRACTICE'."

"These are the Float Pool nurses".

109

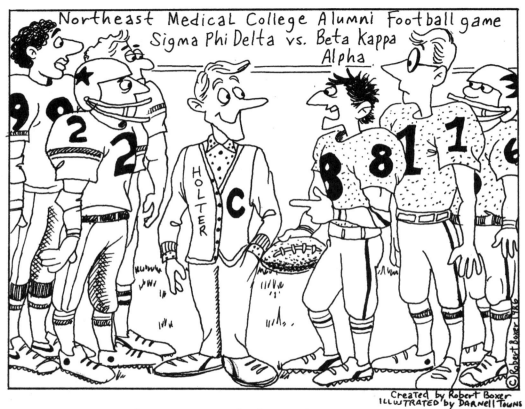

"We want the cardiologist, Sam Holter, to coach us since he's an expert on 'Beta Blockers'."

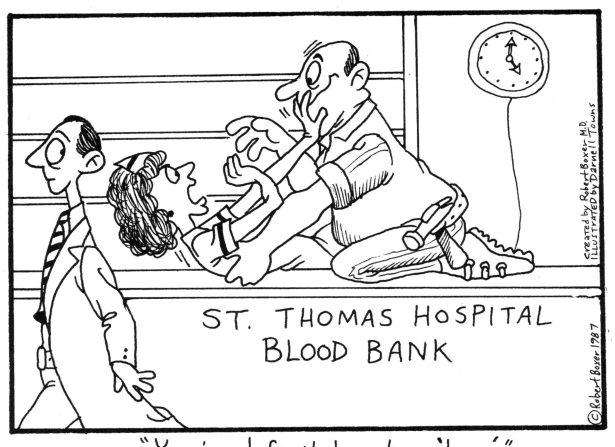

"You're definitely not my 'type'."

"We recommend that we put our orthopedic surgeon in charge of casting."

"Hey doc, I heard you're great at helping patients get rid of Ticks."

"I can't believe it, I thought that when God made you, he threw away the mold."

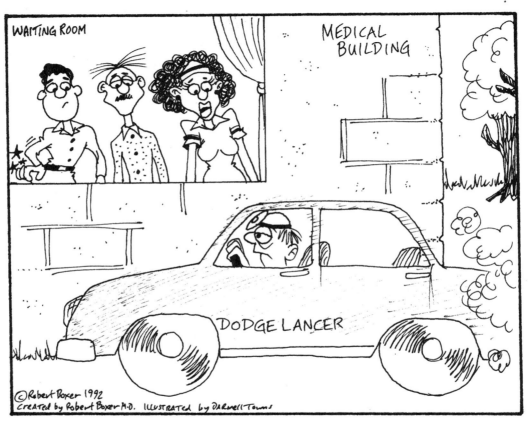

"THE WAIT IS OVER. HERE COMES DR. PETERS
TO INCISE YOUR BOILS."

created by Robert Boxer M.D. ILLUSTRATED BY DARNELL TOWNS

"The Chairman of the department likes all studies to be double-blinded".

"My doctor said I couldn't change my Genes but I fooled him."

119

"EVER SINCE HE WAS A KID HE'S HAD AN INTEREST IN OFFSHORE DRILLING."

"I suppose you want Armours Thyroid"?

121

`Doctor, can you patch test my doll to cabbage;

"I'm trying to make a molar solution."

"As a specialist in veterinary psychology, why is it that you treat so many chinese **wrinkle** dogs?"

"Because they are all chronically **de-pressed.**"

"The Doctor told me to drink plenty of freshly squeezed juice, but not to strain myself".

"I'm glad to see that you finally put your nose to the grindstone".

"I might have to send you to a **Sub** specialist".

128

"There are many Orthopedic surgeons in India, possibly because of the **caste** system".

"Stick around. This orthopedic surgeon is particularly good for humerus occasions."

131

"Hey Doc, Now's a good time to buy that **Overhead** protection policy."

'No, this is not what is meant by a Rotation Diet.'

"This is Denvers' sports channel, bringing you the Annual ski jumping competition. We'll be interviewing a prominent orthopedic Surgeon right after this 'Break'."

"It's superstition with him. He always takes **four-sips** in case it turns out to be a difficult delivery".

"You can see this is a Refereed Journal."

"Since you are a famous immunologist, would you like a B-cell or a T-cell?"

"WHAT A COINCIDENCE, WE WERE JUST YESTERDAY DISCUSSING "CORN ON THE COBB."

"My patient wants to know
the expiration date of these placebos."

141

"Doc, if it's true that your body is your temple, then I want to change religions".

Carpool Tunnel Syndrome

A Knight In Armour

"THESE ARE ALL PATIENTS WITH MENIERES SYNDROME, THEY HEARD THE BEST SPIN DOCTORS ARE IN THE WHITE HOUSE."

"I appreciate the fact that you can type, but can you also cross match?"

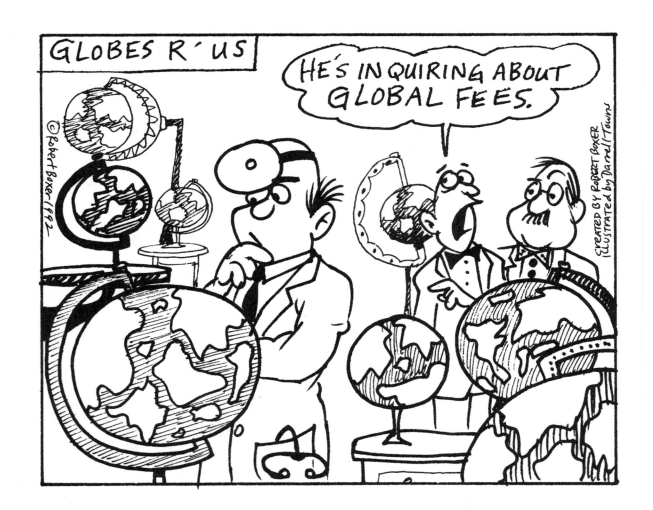

"THIS IS NOT EXACTLY WHAT I HAD IN MIND WHEN I ASKED ABOUT A SHRINK WRAPPER."

"Relax, I don't want your money. I just want the Over-The-Counter medications."

"Don't worry, Officer. This is just part of a Tissue Transplantation program.

153

"Now you're really splitting Hairs!"

"I think this Organ transplantation program
is a wonderful idea".

155

"The Medical director is upset because this New doctor has diagnosed everyone as having a Miner lung problem."

Doctor #1 "I think our patient is slipping!"
Doctor #2 "Peddle faster, he's about to go in-seine!"

"Honey, when your cardiologist said you needed a Pacemaker, I'm sure that he didn't mean this."

"I can't go in there with you. My doctor
said I'm allergic to second hand tobacco smoke."

160

"Just because the doctor ordered occult blood tests doesn't mean he suspects you're a psychic."

163

"OH, THAT MUST BE THE WEEKEND SKELETON CREW."

"No, for a second opinion, I need another obstetrician/ gynecologist, not a labor negotiator."

"I wish they would come up with a "Cordless baby".

"Don't worry... my golfing partner is the judge and he's very familiar with my handicap".

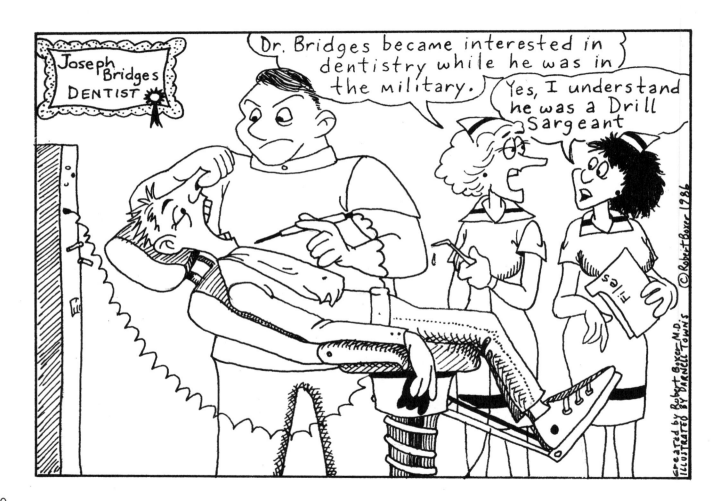

"Mrs. Conception, the jury has found you guilty. You are hereby sentenced to two days of hard labor."

"She's been struggling with shingles for six months now".

"Darnell, you should take a break. It seems like you're going over the EDGE."

"I can see that this party is paid for by the Hospital's slush fund."

"Yeah doc, the pressure is mounting".

175

"Dr. Smith just left, he's headed out to our satellite office today".

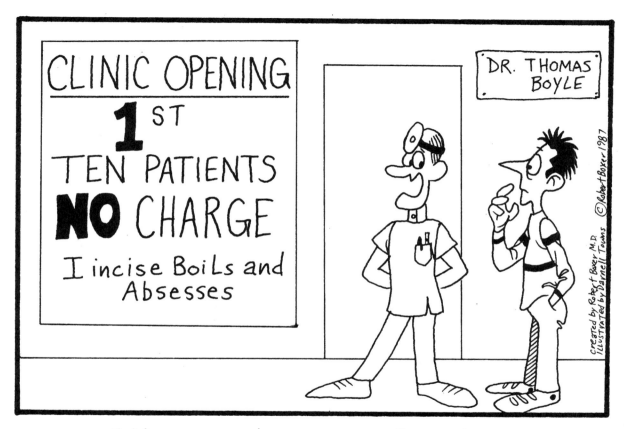

"You might say I'm free lancing."

Gazelle Institute of Human Behavior.

"Yeah doc, I do feel kind of Spacey."

179

"It's for sure Dr. Tardy is not specializing in 'wait' reduction".

"Careful Len, don't make a spectacle of yourself."

182

183

"You're right, doctor. Since the operation, I'm not as hoarse as I used to be."

Acknowledgments

(The Guilty Parties)

For encouragement and support of the creative ? process that led to this collection of pun cartoons, I'm especially indebted to: good friends Bill and Zehavah Frankel for painstakingly reviewing all of the cartoons, as they did for our previous book. Bill and Zehavah are not only good friends, but Bill is a copyright attorney as well, and his advice has again been invaluable; good friend Nancy Janus, and Marcia Steinberg, both of whom typed descriptions of many of the cartoons and made comments and helpful suggestions.

Additionally, support and encouragement, both past and present, were provided by a number of colleagues, relatives, and friends, including the following: Doctors Carl Davis Jr., Eugene Goldman, Wayne Wirtz, Renee Reich, Lenny Berlin, Michael Lewis, Larry Maillis, Arnie Swerdlow, Arkady Rapoport, Sushil Sharma, Bernie Hankin, David Lee, Pat Ebenhoeh, Joe LaMothe, Bruce Berkson, Steven Meyers, Stuart Meyer, Naphtali Gutstein, Coleman Seskind, Alon Winnie, Tom Stone, Allan Lieberman, William Rea, Ken Gerdes, Mort Teich, David Buscher, Charlie Hinshaw, Frank Waickman, Rich Hrdlicka, Wayne Konetzki, Bill Kerr, Jim Holland, Keith Sarpolis, Emily Gottlieb, Shirley Forbes, Mick Meiselmann, Ira Bernstein, Bill Fagman, Jack Isaacs, Paul Bubala, Larry Elegant, Charlie Swarts, Herb Greenfield, Len Drucker, Kenneth Krischer, George Burica, Doris Rapp, Stuart Oserman, Jerry Bernstein, Doug Cook, Joel Sanders, Jerold Miller, Herbert Lippitz, Harold Shafter, Dave Fretzin, Don Ziegler, Marianne Budzeika, Gene and Joan Meyer, Eva Olech, Suellyn Rossman, Joel Klein, Robert LaPata, Dolly Thomas, Tony Daddono, Hugh Falls, Leigh Rosenblum, Phil Krause, Frank Kelly, and Martin Kaplan.

Others that have been supportive include the following: Rose Levin (my mother-in-law), Ord Matek, A.C.S.W., an author and neighbor, Shelly and Elliot Abramson, Ann Marie Pryde, Verne Bengtson, Jim and Carolyn Snorek, Eric Boxer, Russell Boxer (my godson and very clever heir apparent punster), Martin Boxer, Jack and Helen Boxer, Joyce Heitler (a remarkably creative and innovative teacher, public relations expert, and organizer of the highly successful and entertaining annual Punsters Dinner in Chicago), Gregory Opelka, Ron Siegel, Anita Siegel, Tony Placzek, Marcia Placzek, Carol Hopwood, Bud and Georgia Photopulos, Esther Yochim, Jennifer Diehl, Colleen Spagnola, Jean Elliott, Kay Samec, Stacy Sochacki, John Frigo, Lucille Selans, Judy Kaplan, Avery DeLott, David Hochman, Karyn, Marcy, and Alan Gilbert, Howard and Sheila Pizer, Marjorie Hurt Jones, Marjorie Fisher, Diane Kubis, Lynn and Court Lawson, Andrew Fisher, Nick Mechales, Scott Friedrich (one of the youngest and cleverest riddle makers), Dick Boylan, Joe Bobak, Joe Bobak, Jr., Danny Bobak, Tom Kretler, Dan Hales, John Eisenbart, Chris Moriarty-Field and Mark Field, George Carpenter, Sol Bloom, Barbara Kravets, Bonnie Minsky, Sam Rabin, Karen Eness, Jack and Devorah Isaacs, Scott Lewis and Camille Wittig, Linda Forman, Rachel Forman, Carole Isaacs, Gail Krischer, Jack and Fran Mabley, June Winnie, John Yeh and Teresa A. Reilly, Ed and Lisa Stein, Susan Jahnke, Connie Tschudy, Linda Balogh, Jeanne Esposito, Diane Plennert, Marie Burns, and Marci Good.

Especially supportive have been: Bob Herguth, columnist for the Chicago Sun Times, and Dr. Gary Oberg, and his nurse, Jan Beima, who by laughing at my puns at some medical meetings, have intentionally or unintentionally encouraged me to continue.

I'm especially indebted to my wife, Marsha, and to my son, Richard, who is a physician, and who has frequently made creative comments and very helpful suggestions. I am also grateful to my other son, Stephen, who works with me in our office, and who has been an invaluable aid in so many ways. Since our last book has been published, I'm fortunate enough to have the added support of a terrific daughter-in-law, Lisa (Stephen's wife) and her parents, Barbara and Larry Soibel.

My two year old grandson, Jake, fortunately doesn't understand puns yet (he eventually will), but he is very cute and precious and entertaining and amusing and also helps to keep me in a humorous and loving mood.

To all of these very dear people, and to all those inadvertently omitted, I am deeply appreciative of your support and encouragement, but please remember that many of you are guilty of aiding and abetting a punster!

About the Author

Dr. Robert W. Boxer is a practicing allergist, with offices in the Professional Building of the Old Orchard Center in Skokie, Illinois, a suburb of Chicago. Bob has created thousands of pun cartoons, and many have been illustrated by Darnell Towns. For four years, pun cartoons incorporating the themes of medicine and sports appeared regularly in *THE MAIN EVENT*, *A MONTHLY SPORTS JOURNAL FOR PHYSICIANS*. Bob's first book, *Boxer Shorts, More Than Just A Brief Attempt At Humor*, also illustrated by Darnell Towns, was published in 1988. The second book, *Boxer Shorts, Round 2, More Than Just A Brief Attempt At Humor*, also illustrated by Darnell Towns, was published in 1994.

After graduating from Southwest High School in Kansas City, Missouri, Bob earned his Pre-Medical Degree at the University of Denver. He then obtained his Medical Degree from Northwestern University Medical School, served his internship and residency at Cook County Hospital in Chicago, and trained in allergy at the University of Illinois College of Medicine in Chicago. Currently, he is on the medical staffs at Lutheran General Hospital in Park Ridge, Illinois, and Rush North Shore Medical Center in Skokie, Illinois. He is a Fellow of The American Academy of Allergy, Asthma, and Immunology, The American College of Allergy, Asthma, and Immunology, The American Association of Board Certified Allergists, The Illinois Society of Allergy, Asthma, and Immunology, and The American Academy of Environmental Medicine. Dr. Boxer is a member of The American Medical Association and The Illinois State and Chicago Medical Societies. He is on the Professional Advisory Board of the "Nutrition For Optimal Health Association", and is a member of Alpha Omega Alpha Honor Medical Society. Bob was named Punster of the Year by the International Save The Pun Foundation in 1993.

About the Illustrator

(Written by the Artist)

Darnell Towns began drawing at the age of three. Under the tutelage of his brother, John, he was able to hone his drawing ability. At the age of five, he realized he wanted to be a cartoonist when he grew up. Darnell graduated from the School of the Art Institute of Chicago with a B.F.A. in Film Making and Animation. Shortly after graduation, Darnell was searching through the School of the Art Institute's job placement book and found a Robert W. Boxer, M.D. who needed someone to illustrate his puns for a series of books. Well, Darnell answered the ad and the rest is history.

Currently Mr. Towns is an instructor at the Illinois Institute of Art in Chicago where he teaches students how to create cartoon characters and how to story board ideas for future film projects.

List of Carttoons

1. Auto Immune Disease
2. Shrink Wrapper
3. Middle Of A Bridge
4. Tablets I Told You To Take
5. Speed Limit Thirty Five
6. Book Of French Impressionists
7. We're Really Swamped
8. Re-Fur-Ral
9. Lost My Crown
10. Diplomatic Immunity
11. Frozen Section
12. Ghost Surgery
13. No Fluke
14. Charlatan
15. Low Key Office
16. Manipulate To The Top
17. Great Gag Gift
18. Projectile Vomiting
19. Sex Symbol
20. Mood Elevator
21. Float This Week
22. Wastebasket Diagnosis
23. Excellent Foot Notes
24. Hospitals Merge
25. Change Of Heart
26. Hare Analysis
27. Starts With T3 and T4
28. Mercury Poisoning
29. Expert On Unbundling
30. My Mother Encysted
31. Special Delivery Stamps
32. Niacin Flush
33. Sample Rooms
34. Not Your Average Crock
35. Vitamin B Complex
36. Diaper Rash
37. Second Opinion
38. Become Important
39. Therapeutic Trial
40. Disc Problems
41. Piece Of Cake
42. FBI Mole
43. Seats In The C-Section
44. Swallows Come Back To Capistrano
45. Butterfly Collection
46. Status Asthmaticus
47. Hospital Turf Battle
48. M.D.s Were Defeated
49. Terminal Illness
50. Two Boxes Of Tissue
51. Red Zinger
52. Precarious
53. Tick Doc
54. Global Fee
55. Hang Ups
56. PET Scanner
57. Satellite Office
58. Mind Boggling
59. Fearful Of Rejection
60. Cello Mold
61. Pier Review
62. Freudian Slip

125. Not To Strain Myself
126. Nose To The Grindstone
127. Subspecialist
128. Low Pressure Area
129. Caste System
130. Humerus Occasions
131. Thinks The World
132. Use This Hourglass
133. Overhead Protection Policy
134. Rotation Diet
135. Ski Jumping
136. Candy From A Baby
137. Four Sips
138. Refereed Journal
139. B-cell or T-cell
140. Corn On The Cob
141. Date Of Placebos
142. Body Is Your Temple
143. Carpool Tunnel Syndrome
144. Knight In Armour
145. Spin Doctors In White House
146. Army Induction Center
147. A Little Culture
148. Also Cross Match?
149. Studying Subconscious
150. Global Fees
151. Shrink Wrapper
152. Over The Counter Medications
153. Tissue Transplantation
154. Splitting Heirs
155. Organ Transplantation

156. Miner Lung Problem
157. Go In-Seine
158. Pacemaker
159. Second Hand Tobacco Smoke
160. On His Culture
161. Occult Blood
162. Cursory Examination
163. Another Slow Fib
164. Weekend Skeleton Crew
165. Shrimp And The Crab
166. Labor Negotiator
167. Impunity
168. Cordless Baby
169. My Handicap
170. Drill Sergeant
171. Two Days Hard Labor
172. Struggling With Shingles
173. Over The Edge
174. Hospital Slush Fund
175. Pressure Mounting
176. Head To Satellite Office
177. Free Lancing
178. Gazelle Institute
179. Feel Kind Of Spacey
180. Wait Reduction
181. Spectacle Of Yourself
182. Off The Wall
183. Goose Bumps
184. Not As Hoarse
185. Inhaler Just Ran Out